# Brink

Jo Burns

Brink

First published 2021

Turas Press
6-9 Trinity Street
Dublin D02 EY47
Ireland.
info@turaspress.ie
www.turaspress.ie

British Library Cataloguing Data
A CIP catalogue record for
this book is available from the British Library.

ISBN: 978-1-913598-24-2

Cover image: Gustav Klimt's *Der goldene Apfelbaum*
Photo reproduction Shutterstock, extended licence for commercial use.
Cover design by Angie Crowe
Interior typesetting by Printwell Design, Dublin 3
Printed in Ireland by SPRINTprint

# CONTENTS

*Für meine Kinder*

*No one hears howling dogs, or fate's footsteps.*

**Wisława Szymborska**

# The Time it Takes, Revisited

Only a minute to spread false facts or a day
to seed dreams of new regimes. Only an hour
to cast a vote or a week to see propaganda spin.

Only a week to plan murmurs on the street
or a month to group on social media, a season
to entirely change your colours,

as you strut on the brink with extremists.
A year to debunk experts, with the right
agenda. Under 90 years for blind mechanics

to wind watches back to 1933. Three generations
to replicate old, feathered nests of fear and panic.
Some sentences take only five seconds to say,

like Let's never repeat history. You will
believe in silence and think that's all long gone,
but it takes only one swing of the cuckoo clock.

# Truth

If we let a word just slip away
on leader's orders, if it's erased,
an important word, and if we obey
and it slips into nowhere, and if the weight
of history drops it and every day
explosions of gaslight bury us slowly
and the machines have us holed up,
wary, as empty language digs our grave
and the word disappears before we notice,
will we have anything of depth left to say
other than, we thought and prayed?

# Epiphany at the Testing Station

God, you've us plagued, in a line of cars,
QR codes scanned, offering our throats

to a faceless man. The future's a bow,
taut, like apocalypse, and how it reverbs.

Here comes Apollo, gloved, with his silver
arrows, joking at the state of us, while

he draws the swab. It's minute, on a scale,
yet huge. I'm released for now. Oh God,

of divine and hallowed distance, the radio
rasps, infectious with talk of the soul

of America. From the grave risen,
my incantation is a smile, not to any gods

dead or living but for small human graces,
which, in my book, will always save us.

# Zoom

It's History class and my daughter gossips
in the chat box. The topic is Kristallnacht.
I can hear it from the kitchen, on the phone
to Northern Ireland, reminiscing
with a friend about a boy I fancied
at fifteen. He pulled a balaclava on
and stormed class with a water pistol.
The teacher screamed *Save yourselves!*
We laugh about it 30 years later.
Now, my daughter twists her hair
around her finger, with some filter on.
The young teacher has outdone himself
but she's focussed on his smile. Oh, child
of mine, I once was you, so oblivious
to politics, everything a teenage joke,
unaware of living time that will, one day,
be in books. And will never leave you.

# Zoonose

I will tell my grandchildren how we hoarded soap
when disinfectant became gold dust, how shelves

emptied, and life became much simpler
as we were forced to shed the unnecessary; flights,

concerts, we could have halved our carbon footprint.
At first it seemed like one beautiful chance to heal

a bursting world, shrunk to the size of our closest.
But we forgot; time isn't linear, rather a circle.

# Terminarch

*For Fatu, Kenya, 2018*

Girl, you're the last combination of chromosomes
and randomly smolt genes of your species.

You wear survival on your hide like an armour
of melted-down spearheads and machetes.

You vocalize the thunderous gutterals
of your indigenous tongue into seasons of hollow,

and are last to walk the way of the pilgrims
and mates to the familial watering holes.

Your brothers crossed the Ngorongoro cradle
to the other side to join the djinn. Their fathers,

and fathers before them, travelled past
the cauldron caldera that you would call home,

if free to. Their pride graces marble and teak tresors
as polished handles of yemenese daggers,

or ground to myth in apothecary powders.
But your grandfather, as rare as rhodium

in his life, cleared the walls of hunting lodges,
reverse-engineering evolution

to a crash of poems. Like you, he was a birth
of magma from the fertile crater core.

Now receding like lava back to the spirits,
he is a zip of unravelling DNA helix

and nucleotides you share but have no use for.
As you search through cracks of crust and mantle

for the rest of your days, some holy place
to call your own, you lumber on petered-out trails

of seed and sequence, relic and reason,
red dust. You are from, yet also filled with, volcano

and desire for something with no name, no outlet.
You are so many things at once, a matriarch

without fold, an endling of magical code,
revered by the old ones, in lineage and bone.

And the horizon is a blood sky spilling towards
you. Fatu, you're extinct despite still living

and we mourn the last ever male of your kind,
the northern white rhino, named Sudan,

who leaves you, granddaughter, behind him.

# On the Brink

*2018 B.C.*

I send my soldiers before the mules,
Carthaginians and 37 elephants.
The alpine folk, warned of caravans

are whipped by starving grunts and snarl.
They dig graves in glaciers, carve the paths
to allow mammoth cabals over the pass.

All stripped bare on perilous rock and ice,
these are my concerns going up:
Which route will take us to fresh lakes and food?

I feel small and mortal. How long
do we need, what relief is ahead? I'm desperate
to see what the months will bring.

*2018 A.D.*

I send our group ahead and go back
to drag my alp-virgin parents over the pass.
2000 years in the seconds I lace up my boots

in a Tyrolean hut. Our backpacks full
of Compeed and wine, we take selfies
at the border sign. Trekking poles preserve

what melting glaciers would snatch from us.
These are my concerns, going down, on scree:
Which route will bring my elephants home?

I feel immense, yet out of control.
There is no snow, so we'll be back by tea
as we teeter on the Anthropocene.

# Octaves of Rain

*Germany, Spring 2020*

The thunder booms Mussorgsky
tension over the corrugated iron roof, lines
of silver from gullied grooves as notes
are stretched to crystal strings.
Now the garden cathedral rises up, gothic,
as grass incense swings its botafumeiro
and petrichor weaves through vertical opera.
Nascent bass plays it all dark indigo blue.

*Lower Base Camp 2010*

The last time I heard rain pound so hard,
I lay near Buddha, under a bursting cloud
as mudslides shrouded our tour-guide's mantra.
It never rains in Ladakh he'd said over and over.
We'd chanted it so often it became our rosary
and we must have angered Chang La gods.
Stok Kangri and Indra let loose in fury,
shooting mud crescendos down the pass.

*Leh 2010*

Morning burial, borne of Markha dust,
innocent sky, baby blue, palest orange,
silent, but for one lonely radio playing
on repeat: Om mane padme hum.
Whirrs of helicopter blades approached us
as soldiers dug up children, cars and buses
to lay their lost in striped Tibetan blankets,
the rain dried into lists of the dead,

the yak wool soaked and bleeding.

# Smuggling Apples

*For Irena Sendlerowa (codename Jolanta).*

Picture this: Beside *Jurisprudence,*
Klimt's Golden Apples is engulfed
when the SS detonate

a castle full of plunder, as they flee
*Schloss Immendorf.* And you and I,
transported, cast a final look

at the canvas, bearing witness.
Under branches we'd hope to find
*Aigle, Hesperia, Arethusa,*

the dancing nymphs and maids,
guarding jewels while they sing
among the green and gold in flames.

*

Here, I'd digress to talk about
an apple tree, a secret backyard,
deep in Warsaw. Buried

in the tomb of night, a pickling jar
could be unearthed, screwed tight
with names and code addresses,

listing over 2000 children
decades younger. Now immortal
apples, ripe, unstolen.

\*

Let's speak of borders, foresight, prudence;
how caging skies hold Eden under.
I'll reveal a Polish nurse,

a simple woman with a garden,
smuggling carts of tools and babies,
piled linen sacks for older children.

She trains her dog to bark
to hide the cries from uniform.
*Teresa, Yoram, Piotr, Michal, Katarczyna.*

*

Now we're back in *Immendorf,*
watching Klimts from years before,
collapse and blacken in the flames

as jurisprudence falls asunder.
No hundred-headed dragon,
*Ladron.* Just a huddled woman

in the shadows with her tools,
her drugs and sacks, passing guards
at ghetto gates, and for a moment,

just a beat, Jolanta's caught
but blind men shrug and let her pass,
dog howling, while she sings.

# Maembe

*Kinacholeta ugomvi duniani ni kugawanya nyama*
*The cause of dispute in the world is the distribution of meat*

A Suzuki, with goat tied on pillion,
overtakes us after leaving Njombe.
The jeep limps as we approach a village
where a crowd sing the *Karibu Asana* greeting.
My host raises six daughters alone
(husband dead of that unspoken disease)
and she's prepared a banquet: Ugali, chard
from Iringa market, and green beans.
And more; my dinner got here first.
Wide eyes devour the slaughtered feast.
Mama, in her best Kanga, shoos them off
*This is what Mzungu gets to eat.*
The oldest girl is watching me,
here, where mangoes never ripen past green,
where children hide until the white men sleep
then burst into fields for *Maembe.*
She knows the ritual before each meal,
holds out a towel and jug of water for me
to wash my hands for, and of, this scene.

# Discourse

Lately, I've been thinking of my home
and that of my children, fighting

for my tongue, like soldiers
of the Armada, landing one by one

like crabs to beach in gerundium.
Words are not unlike the men

of the Girona, who knew the Atlantic
carries the world. I imagine them

crawling, blue calls swallowed
by gales, far from natal waters.

I've travelled far from roots
and prefix, to new phonemes

just to learn language is not only
lexis but also a fierce weapon.

There's no revelation. Still, I'll paint
a tale of 1300, raised from shears

at Lacada point, who climb aboard
a galleass of latinate to tack and jibe

away from chimes of Ulster Scots
to recourse journeys made, and time,

to keep what is left within them.

# Attrition

A man said time is the longest distance
between two places. I say tongues.
An accent can save a man or damn him.
A woman can feel her native one
slip away. I dream these days inflected,

German, Spanish sweeping up conviction,
turning back, stretched over seas,
booms and bows swung through the ventus,
breezing routes to common domum,
metered accents drowning stresses,

my dialect sailing wars of discourse
back to where names are a confession,
where English vowels split a nation.
My tongue has always craved *Verbindung,*
a union, homeward bound.

# As the Silent Ones Thought and Prayed

*im Janusz Korczak, children's author and orphanage director in the Warsaw ghetto*

under stars, the songs and stories burnt
to rain-soaked ash and rhythm,
as crunching, too-light feet in snow

were herded, kindling on the platform.
Past the power, black flaming hearts,
they marched to songs of women, children

in the wild lyrics of Treblinka;
a people, embers, sky igniting.
Among it rose a lullaby, so *Kinder*

couldn't hear stones cry, or fire.
As Janusz walked, he sang. The words
aren't known, nor do they matter,

but were kind and at that moment
all of one man's life on offer.
Blue knapsacks stacked below the chorals

of rising beats, thin voices curling
over bags packed full of hope.
In Sunday clothes, they reached the line

of a stanza where past and future go.
A *Kindermärchen* with no ever after,
Janusz is now at the threshold.

His own soft words are the whitest lie,
ablaze, imploding on his shoulders.
Gravity and melody implore

and sing two hundred in.
Janusz, with them in the core,
lights the way while light becomes him.

Left and right, his arms outstretched.

# Forest Bathing

*"Without ceasing the sap rises from its roots, nurturing even the smallest of leaves. Do I hear, perhaps, a secret heartbeat? I press my face against its dark, warm bark and think to myself: homeland"* — Sophie Scholl

Summer always seems to understand
that to make way for the wind is life,
as all we know is turned on its head.

The forest floor is my penumbra and I lie
in remembrance of what trees know
of bloom and clairvoyance.

Low today, in ruffle, the deer are a flash
of tilt and whim. Rustles and echoes pull me
back to youth, melt and discord, how the taste

of the Atlantic is not unlike blood.
Where April's wink glittered troubled loughs,
flirting with rocks, looking down

on the brink of abandon. Years on,
my fingernails are rooted in moss. I'm lying,
bone spread under bone and lately

there's a feel of something repeating
itself. If I could, I'd break through
crust to mantle, I would be heliotrope,

young again, unaware of season
or significance, full of fire and conviction.
Leaves are the middle-aged proof

that light's not definite, that everything
we love is fragile, and all that we know
is dual. Shadows cast, I used to think

discovery is fleeting, only happening
once. But shade and sun are equal concepts,
rise and fall. And rise. Over and over.

# Imaginary Departure Lounges

*2021*

After one year of lockdown, home-schooling
and Zoom, you are dreaming of danger

and flying to some imaginary lover
of all lovers in Santiago, or San Francisco

with a circle of friends (all artists).
You're on a list for a soirée of painting

and absinthe. The masters are all in town.
Awake in the morning, your head is sore

and diamonds are now your bloodshot eyes.
In the liminal between insomnia and sleep,

a volcano of volcanoes with the mother
of all names has drawn vetoes to dream-affairs.

Pipes have burst and your cellar is flooded.
Duty is now pelting ash at your back,

in pulsing morse code. *It's not over.*
*Stay home. Stay home. Stay home.*

# Cooking in the Anthropocene

Student of the next great epoch,
reading this: imagine this poet of forty-four
(at the time) on a Mac book (check
capsules on Mars) thinking of how
to charter years on the down.

We, who emptied the pantries
of neighbours (who foraged,
finally, for nothing) ignored
the headlines. Resourceful as ever,
we tested all the food crazes.

We preached on Facebook, over
and over, about change, so we didn't
actually need to. And when a leader
burnt all the facts, we smouldered
as some posted *Give him a chance.*

# Hoar Frost

Damp haired, in front of the open fire, on beanbags
(one Superman, one Victoria Plum) we are swaddled

in blankets, cereal bowls on our laps loaded
with Maltesers, Fruit Pastilles and Cadbury's Buttons.

I'm craving the A team, my brother Knightrider.
BA Baracus won't get on no plane. Hannibal is donning

black leather gloves as Faceman holsters his colt trooper
magnum. Michael and Kitt are in pursuit of assassins,

our parents in the good room clink Tyrone crystal.
Voices murmur, manoeuvering through each other

in a muffled web, as news bursts through the armour
of Saturday evening, wrapping rime ice

around a blast in an Ulster pub with no inkling,
before supercooling, on our TV screen, to a headline.

# Confusing Protestants and Catholics with Prostitutes and Cowboys

In my defence, it was the cassette in my dad's car,
Greatest Country Hits that had me confused;

Harper Valley PTA's misdefined woman,
socking it to conservatives.

Also family talk of westerns, christians,
Ronald Reagan, bandits, juxtaposed

with the bearded man, muted on the news,
before the opening credits of Dallas.

I was befuddled, like you reading this.
Music and politics inextricably muddled; one side

babbled Gospel, the other side were rebels.
This is a story of childhood misconclusions. See,

for years I thought of Gerry Adams, MP,
on his much-misquoted flight for freedom,

as a cowboy, drinking his vocal chords dry
in Nashville bars or dusty El Paso.

# In the Western Ghats Rubber Plantation

Where once starlings eddied, prattled,
throats thick with bloom in lustrous jade,
the tick-tock of latex taps percussive

to sap tunes, until an uppan calls.
Between grey bark, in this fallout,
he (also called the great coucal)

bronze, magnificent, a chola remnant
has quivers of cobra in his ruby eye.
The mongoose starve. Cormorants

no longer dive, yet he, in yawns
of polymer, looks to the neem bowl below.
His call dims to monotone

coup coup, coup coup, coup coup.
Trees answer in foreign colloid tongues
tap tap, tap tap, tap tap.

In thrall to hollow sounds of slopes,
among caoutchouc trees, the coucal
cocks his ear for any  living  note.

# Undercover

Darling Eli, I fear the worst
as Mossad are avoiding me. I hope
you're with your mistress. Only
I read of how you saw your chances
in the Golan heights, and feigned concern
for Arabs melting on their guns.
You planted eucalyptus gums
in their thousands, evergreen,
so soldiers could cool under them
then passed the note to Tel Aviv.
I received your letter, promising
you'd give it up. But just this week
the IDF have blitzed those trees,
turquoise and Syria betrayed.
Your shade is hanging over us.
One sign of life would be enough.
I'm waiting for your word.

# In the Branches of a Dream

Translation of *Im Geäst des Traumes* by *Horst Lange, 1945*

You saw how everything died,
already at the very start.
Even the boldest colours
faded and sank, worn out.

Your words, they dusted over,
fruitless, now just scrawns of leaves.
Every reflex resembled an old smile,
numb and furrowing.

You knew nothing about yourself,
nothing that can cover, or encompass,
sleep, just the vague stretch of an animal,
that's thrown itself down in tall grass.

The crystal of night bloomed
faraway from your own face.
Voices dimmed to soft and gentle
but you did not escape harsh day.

# The Terminal 1 Smoking Lounge

Funny, how midlife crises start in smoking lounges.
You look done (God's sake, you've no make-up on)

holding your thirty-year lungs up, a flag of tar.
And who'd think, with all the life and bustle outside,

you'd flee into a glass coffin, willingly, for peace?
But you're met with an ashtray vaudeville

as Rodrigo y Gabriela flay MTV
before a New Orleans promo video melts

over a model-slash-artist called Juan.
Places you've never been, oozing over

you, more focused on Pinot Grigio these days,
a mottled old bruise when the kids are in bed.

Delayed and beige, on your way to Belfast,
you inhale the times before you tied the knot

on your tongue. Boarding call. Your husband
and toddlers; your obvious gold in the open.

Matte in a discoball, greed lights you another
to the muffles of Mummy, Come out!

Woman, did you really think you could run
from life? If so, where to? And who from?

# Freefall

Because of the sequential chain
of things, I submerged, my evening
Pinots un-syncopated by female gossip
at the bar. Everything was horizontal
and heavy, a stagnation of status quo.

My eyes darted escapes from masks
in the year, on the circular
timeline, after the tolerant politician,
on his porch voiced the diameter
of open arms. And was silenced.

Then the attack on the synagogue
sent things fluid. In conscious
vendetta, everything amassed, bursting
left to right, in curve, from extremist
to pandemic. I can't dam,

but I will damn these years,
where everything in me splayed
and straightened, flowing vertical,
into drop and voyage of raging
torrents and paralyzed phrases.

The irony and unyielding motion
of the flood that swept us all
off tangent. Passive-Aggressive
on the lip, I write it; brink,
the tilt that we spectated.

# German Autumn

*1946. After Stig Dagerman*

Because the cellars are yawning, the stench
of years and peace is revealing itself
as empty stomachs. Because potatoes
are gold and arbitration is in full flow. Because
the city's alive yet barely breathing. Because
a woman sends her boy to scavenge.
Because a man, who turned his head,
lists who'll speak for his character
for bread. Because the cellar is finally airing
and the trains are spewing those who fled
to the country, back into ash and silence.
Because the city is censored and bound
to a promise and because shame is palpable
on this side of the brink. Because the American
langours at the station. Because the woman
takes flour in exchange for her only currency.
Because the man listens in court, unable
to speak the unspeakable. Because something
has fallen from a purse, a suitcase, a pocket,
the sky. Because someone has fallen,
a father, a grandfather, a brother, pride,
the boy at the station is watching and waiting
for his chance, barefoot in smoking rubble.

# Göring dreams of his brother Albert

*Nuremburg. 1946*

*Ad Hominem*

I dream of our formidable
mother, who believed we become
what we loved when young.

With the certainty of distance,
in my instance, she was wrong.
I loved Epenstein but blazing

words were drugs and call to flight.
At times I feel her pull me back,
when morphine lets me sleep

like you, along the corridor.
My images flow from a secret pen,
replete with poison. Silhouettes

of you, scrubbing cobbles on your knees
with Jewish women, your secret mazes
leading the men I sought to safety.

*Extenuation*

The planes, the camps. I'm swinging
in this twilight towards the flashes
of the alpine sanatorium

where the cult was booming.
New Heilkunde was veiling science,
drawing aristocrats from Munich.

With my soldiers, I was holidayed
for mountain air and rest from service.
The owner/doctor, a hunting friend,

had remedies used by the Führer.
Drawn into duality, I craved
the icy pools and sauna.

I conquered Hochkreuth, after hiking
to catch the swirls of crepuscule
with their brown clouds of moths.

*Defiance*

I march down, again, to cool my veins,
my voice upraised, to warn the *Maedels*,
Eve's slim daughters, Aryan,

knee-high in icy water, in the swarm,
enchanted. Wading to *Volk* lyrics,
they spread their wings, unveiled

like magic, death and song awakened.
My visions are as lucid as dissent,
a chance to sketch it all.

You'll be freed, by names you aided,
at dawn. A footnote in my story,
this is your shadow while you're resting.

The pen is now screwed back, intact.
It's dusk and it is glacial. Glass, between
my bite, is cracked as brown eclipses light.

# Distortion

It wasn't so much what we learned
about the president's cronies, more how we stared through
looking glasses on friends and family

and it wasn't even how we suddenly knew
everything about vaccines. It was more, the fact
that, over wine, you skewed and slanted,

fired up and conspiratorial. You toppled
something and I'm torn, because I'm loathe
to let things split. I know othering, and danger,

risks of being sure. I know the mindset.
I know division. One more glass and the fracture
is immutable. You light a cigarette and preach –

forgive me as I note it for a poem –
*our government are terrorists.* You drop the ü berbomb:
*In a past life, I'm sure that I was Sophie Scholl.*

# The Conspiracy

*We, the system critics, are ebbing, onto the streets.*

Some want the Chancellor tried at the Hague
while some hate masks and some just hate.

*We know that in a free country, with free speech,*
*we can say that it's a dictatorship*

Doctors look on, as Jerusalem Challenges are used
as proof of no patients in Telegram Channels
.

*We fight for language of the heart, not reason.*

Some write their own news for 10 cents a day
and you can read the world however you want it.

*As patriots, the chambers of our hearts are red hot.*

The importance is critical mass, not class
and so the group call themselves "Das Volk".

# Fission

In the group's telegram channel   the friend

I lost

       shows herself          lifting her pseudonym

after six months down

                    the rabbit hole


I watch the dots blink          as      she     types

*Lieber bin Ich Nazi als Grün*        I rage

and rub illusions      from my eyes        to witness

*this*
            hate     in plain view

      She'd rather be a Nazi than a Green party voter.

# The Opposite of Enlightenment

*After Mong Lan*

What if we scream *The earth is flat*
and what if deliverance crashes
through the twenties, swaddled
in flags, citing Revelations?
Even when science is repeated
for the millionth time. Even
the orange peel maps or charts
of Magellan, theories of Newton
and Galileo, astronomers' scribbles,
pictures from NASA, not least
neuro-images of how we've evolved.
What is true distance if not measured
by curves between Darwin and carbon
dating? Without gravity, what is light
that won't be unstraightened
between Polaris and Orion?

# Lockdown Terminal 1 Algorithm

Because one of the worlds I lived in
was convex, a pane above cumulus,
cirrus and stratus,

in this algorithm, input imaginary planes,
another country, a woman who may
or may not go by my name.

If terminals are as finite
as oceans, go to her missing the remote
cramp of home province.

Let *Friends* be her go-to,
when dream-continental
and go to a Pinot on the tray.

Input the tube of the dreamers
with no way home, awash
with alcohol. Let the sky be indigo

and Europe, below, a jigsaw
and still pieces of a whole.
If 10,000 metres is vantage,

go to all the meanings
of terminal and pilgrim.
If security finds her undangerous,

go to epiphanies that
home's more than landing.
Let her discover how to decode.

# Abstractions in the Cellar

P.O.W.

       Put to work. Siberia.

            *Abgemagert*. Stalingrad.

                  *Wehrmacht*. Obligated.


Rear Gunner. RAF.

       Birds Eye. Burning Dresden.

       Tail End Charlie.

            Shot. Down. Operated.


*Gauleiter*. SA fighter.

       *Hohes Tier*. Dug up letter.

           Brown Shirt. Stormtrooper.

               *Nazi ID*. Arbitrated.


             Ancestors.

                 Repudiate it.

# Split

I'm on my knees,
with a tub of chalk
in a Bavarian town
stones in remembrance
I'm ridiculous
dressed down in black
My children weren't born
for this place
You get that
*If you're walking*
*you're walking*
Old friend

a Saturday night
plus a list of slogans
cobbled with gold
for those taken
in middle-aged fervour
out past the curfew
for fucking fascists
I made a home
which you tolerate
*with Nazis*
*the wrong way*
Let that rub off

# Umschlagplatz

*i.m Stefania Wilczynska, orphanage director in the Warsaw Ghetto*

Maybe you step back from this place,
called sudden turn. The East is the end.
You drop the hands of two orphans, and back
through the door, retracing the telegraph
to Geneva's Red Cross. *I refuse to leave them.*
You unravel your stitches which clothed them
and, eyes shut, return to Liège. Behind you is
is a flood of salt water, but your mind has to pour
it into emaille. There's no one left to heal.

As there's no one left to heal your mind pours it all
into emaille. Behind you is a flood of salt water
and, eyes shut, you return to Liège, away from
each stitch with which you clothed them.
*I refuse to leave them* unravels as the telegraph
to Geneva's Red Cross leaves through the door,
retracing the hands of two orphans. It's a sudden
turn but the East will be your end and so
you spin and flee this godforsaken place.

# Go into the night

Translation of *Geh in die Nacht* by *Horst Lange, 1948*

Forget the house, forget the room.
Run along fences to where the fields begin.
Forget your name and whatever you are,
repel yourself and plunge into
the night full of longing and fear.
Remember, how the earth bears you,
just as it bears the plants and trees.

Look around, see everything as new.
Go into mist, the breath of rivers
and meadows. Already, lost time blows
like chaff off of you, the years
of nothing but being alone.
Remember, as well as painting the fruit,
how the earth dyed your own blood red.

Lift up your head and tilt your face.
Green light stuns your gaze and you can name
them: Cassiopeia, Orion and the bear.
They aim at your heart, with harm,
love and hate, while they slowly burn.
Remember, that you will nourish the earth,
just as the earth nourished you.

# Lebensfuge

*After Zuzana Rûzicková*

I dreamt I could no longer sing
except in chambers, or faceless groups.

But the music weighed nothing,
undetected and safe, inside

me where no one knew
it existed. It couldn't be stolen.

*What would Bach do?* I asked
as they were all taken away.

Years later, now in Pilsen,
I'm given to prisoner T345,

no longer the daughter
of the toy store owner.

She adapts again to walking solo,
instead of hounded mobs of 5.

Her fingers are twisted, tips
long dead, and find my keys, to span

12 hours a day. My pegs and strings
readjust as D minor bursts

my shortsides. I am old,
a cembalo. I dream, of men

laying stones upon my body,
mazes, wires detecting chords

in my inner, snowy roads
strewn with burnt compositions,

the iron voice of axes, backbones
breaking. But my case is bucking

as she, a broken bird, awakes
me with Bach's kiss of life.

# Origin

Imagine healing
as a dot,

around which mankind
once revolved,

paradise linked to navel,
that mystic bud

that axis mundi,
the nail driven into

Mecca's Ka'ba floor
on which men transcended

prayer. Stripped,
cleansed in Adam's house,

they searched for heaven
on that hot pierce

of stigmata, feeling unity
and forever,

knowing *this* is enough.
It's all there is.

# Election night

Why are you still underwater?
*I've been diving, illuminating the wreck*

Is the citadel still brimming with gold?
*It's now coming down with skeletons.*

Why are you clasping onto feelings of breath?
*Who knows how long exhalation can last?*

Swim up, dizzy, to glints of sapphires.
*A relief of cabochons. Might be fake.*

Do you think you can end, for now, on this image?
*It's liminal. But, my God, I'll take it.*

# Zoonose 2.0

I mentioned time isn't linear, rather
a circle and the story now spins on its own.

I'll tell my grandkids how a policeman took
his knee off a throat, we were immune

to hate, the world held us and it was requited.
I'll tell them we re-bred the white rhinos,

relearnt the discourse of native forests,
left the pangolins in peace. For now, I leave

this to show some wanted to make it better.
Yet want is such a passive verb. Children

of my children, blood of my blood, you are hope,
there will always be something to love.

# March

The populist's open-mic is on
and the crowd is waving *Reichsbürger* flags.
Someone is harping on about vaccines,

Gates, reptilian overlords,
and of course 5G and Rothschild.
I meet up for the first time

with a friend, since the lockdown.
We've the same intention, to spectate
a farce, the one our kids are facing.

But we're happy, despite the distance,
sitting together, in our mission.
We pop too many corks and *prost*

on the pier, above the rabbit hole,
tipsy, dangling over murky water.
Summer's coming but we're split,

conspiracy or truth. And who's to say
which is which or even who is who?
I've lived division in my youth.

Now I face the moon expanding
with a breath that's not my own,
in a land that's not my home.

We are witnesses. Whatever comes.

# Notes

*Terminarch*: Fatu, and her mother, are the last living Northern White Rhinos. Scientists are attempting to rebreed the species using collected sperm from the deceased male rhino Sudan, and IVF.

*Smuggling Apples:* Codenamed Jolanta, Irena was a Polish nurse who smuggled Jewish children from the ghettoes, providing them with false documents and shelter in convents, orphanages or families. She withstood torture and refused to reveal the identities or whereabouts of these children. She was recognized by the state of Israel as Righteous Among the Nations.

*While the Silent Majority Thought and Prayed*: Born Henryk Goldsmit, Janusz Korczak (author name) was a Polish children's author and pedagogue. He spent many years running an orphanage in Warsaw. He repeatedly refused sanctuary, to stay with his orphans. He insisted on accompanying the children to the very end. Every year, on children's day, Warsaw schools visit his monument.

*Undercover:* Eli Cohen was an Israeli spy, working in Syria. Syrian counterintelligence eventually uncovered him and sentenced him to death by hanging in 1965.

*In the Branches of a Dream and Go Into the Night*: Horst Lange, married to Oda Schaefer, was a German poet who published during the Third Reich. He was a proponent of Inner Emigration. His work was categorized as magic realism.

*German Autumn:* A Swedish journalist and writer, Stig Dagerman wrote the book *German Autumn* in 1946. This was lauded by Henning

Mankell as "One of the best collections ever written about the aftermath of war."

*Göring Dreams of his Brother Albert:* Hermann Epenstein, of Jewish descent, was the godfather of Hermann and Albert Göring, and reported lover of Hermann Göring's Mother. It was rumored that he was the biological father of Albert Heilkunde: Natural Medicine was fiercely propagated by the regime as scientific experts were routinely denounced.

*The Opposite of Enlightenment:* Lines two to four are loosely based on a quote by Sinclair Lewis.

*Umschlagplatz:* Stefania Wilczynska worked together with Janusz Korczak at the Warsaw orphanage. She declined to leave Poland following the Nazi invasion. Stefania also accompanied the children from Umschlagplatz, where they were herded together for transport, to the Treblinka gas chambers. This poem imagines a different future for Stefania, if she had left Umschlagplatz. The German verb 'umschlagen' can mean to 'turn over, back or around'.

*Lebensfuge:* Zuzana Rûzicková, from Czechoslovakia, was imprisoned in Theresienstadt, Auschwitz and later Bergen-Belsen. After liberation she became the first harpsichordist to record Johann Sebastian Bach's complete works for keyboard. Her life story is published under the title *Lebensfuge.*

*March:* Reichsbürger (Reich Citizens) is a label for those who reject the legitimacy of the modern German state.

# Acknowledgements

With gratitude to the editors and judges of the following journals and competitions in which these poems appeared:

## Competitions

*Terminarch*: Winner of Listowel Writers' Week Single Poem Competition, judged by Peter Sirr. Shortlisted for An Post Irish Book Awards Poem of the Year 2020.

*Terminal 1 Smoking Lounge*: Poetry News (Truth), judged by Carolyn Jess-Cooke. Winner of the Poetry Society Hamish Canham Prize 2020.

*Hoar Frost*: Poetry Society: Poetry News (Vision) for National Poetry Day, judged by Moniza Alvi.

*Undercover*: Shortlisted for the Plough Poetry Prize judged by Pascale Petit.

## Publications

*Banshee, Cormorant, Four x Four, Lakeview International Journal of Literature* and *Arts, Rascal, Pendemic, The High Window, The Moth* and the pamphlet *Circling for Gods* (Eyewear, 2018).

*Go into the Night (Geh in die Nacht)* and *In the Branches of a Dream (Im Geäst des Träumes)* are translations and adaptations of poems by Horst Lange from *Gedichte aus Zwanzig Jahren*, 1948, Piper Verlag, München.

With thanks to my MFA poetry group, for feedback and inspiration. Special thanks to Alastair Hesp, Audrey Molloy, Eleanor Hooker, Elizabeth McSkeane, Helen Mort, Rebecca Goss and Nick Allen.

# Biography

Jo Burns is originally from Northern Ireland. She lives in Germany and is an English Lecturer and translator.

Her poems have appeared in *Oxford Poetry, Poetry Ireland Review, Poetry News, Southword, The Stinging Fly, The Tangerine, Magma* and elsewhere. She won the McClure Poetry Prize 2017 at the Irish Writers Festival CA, the Magma Poetry Competition 2018, the New Irish Writing in Germany Poetry Award 2018, the 2020 Listowel Irish Writers Week Single Poem Prize and the Poetry Society Hamish Canham Prize. She was shortlisted in 2020 for Irish poem of the year. Her debut pamphlet *Circling for Gods* was published by Eyewear Publishing. Her first collection *White Horses* was published by Turas Press in 2018. She is currently completing an MFA at Manchester Metropolitan University.